high-tech military weapons

COMBAT FIGHTER
F-22
RAPTOR

Steve White

HIGH
interest
books

Children's Press®
A Division of Scholastic Inc.
New York / Toronto / London / Auckland / Sydney
Mexico City / New Delhi / Hong Kong
Danbury, Connecticut

Book Design: Dean Galiano
Book Layout: James Leone
Contributing Editor: Karl Bollers

Photo Credits: Cover, title page, pp. 4, 25, 30 U.S. Air Force; pp. 7, 10, 19, U.S. Air Force/Tech. Sgt. Ben Bloker; p. 8 NASA/Jim Ross; p. 12 Stephen Alvarez/National Geographic Image Collection; pp. 14-15 U.S. Air Force/John Rossino; p. 16 U.S. Air Force/Tech. Sgt. Shane A. Cuomo; p. 18 U.S. Air Force/Darin Russell; pp. 21, 32 U.S. Air Force/Judson Brohmer; p. 23 U.S. Air Force/Staff Sgt. Lanie McNeal; p. 26 U.S. Air Force/Steve White; p. 35 U.S. Air Force; p. 36 U.S. Air Force/Kevin Robertson; p. 39 U.S. Air Force/2nd Lt. William Powell; pp. 44, 45, 46, 48 (background) courtesy Edwards Air Force base

Library of Congress Cataloging-in-Publication Data

White Steve D. (Steve David), 1964
    Combat fighter: F-22 Raptor / Steve White.
    p. cm. - (High-tech military weapons)
    Includes index.
    ISBN-10: 0-531-12090-2 (lib. bdg.)   0-531-18706-3 (pbk.)
    ISBN-13: 978-0-531-12090-3 (lib. bdg.)   978-0-531-18706-7 (pbk.)
    1. F/A-22 (Jet fighter plane)-Juvenile literature. I. Title. II. Series.

    UG1242.F5W45 2007
    623.74'64-dc22

                                                    2006006272

CONTENTS

The F-22 Raptor is a new breed of super-fighter for the twenty-first century.

INTRODUCTION

I t is the middle of the night, and you are flying over the desert. In the cockpit of your F-22 Raptor, the only light you see comes from your radar screen. Even though it's pitch-black outside, you are wearing special goggles that help you see as well as you can in broad daylight. When you look down at your radar again, there are two bright red triangles on it. They are crossing in front of you, moving from left to right. These represent enemy fighters. They are about 200 miles (322 kilometers) away and closing fast.

There's no need to break into a sweat. You are not alone. You have a wingman, flying in another Raptor, 1,000 feet (305 meters) above and behind you. You've trained together and he knows what needs to be done. Suddenly, there is a squeal in your earphones. The enemy's radar is sweeping the skies for you, but it doesn't detect you. You are invisible to them! The enemy fighters pass by and soar off into the night. You turn the Raptor and follow them by using the control near your left hand. You increase the power to the engines using the twin throttles near your right hand. Intense pressure from the turn pushes you back against your seat and down on your lungs. As you level off, the pressure drops. You are flying faster than the speed of sound.

You begin closing in on the enemy fighters. Soon they are only 50 miles (80 km) ahead of you. Your radar tells you how fast they are going and how high they are flying. Computers aboard the Raptor send that information to the computers inside the missiles you are carrying. You lock the missiles onto their targets and fire. They streak through the sky using their own built-in radar to find the enemy fighters.

You look ahead: there are now two flashes in the clouds like distant lightning. The two red triangles disappear from your radar screen. The enemy has been shot down. They never knew they were under attack until it was too late. Mission accomplished.

The F-22 Raptor flies in formation high above the coastline accompanied by a wingman.

The F/A-18 Hornet was among the first fighters built with carbon fiber, making sharp turns in mid-flight possible.

A STAR IS AIRBORNE

During the middle of the twentieth century, fighter planes were made almost entirely out of metals like steel and aluminum. These types of aircraft were heavy and, as a result, not very nimble. In battle, turning too hard would often damage them. All that changed in the 1970s. That's when aircraft manufacturers began using carbon fiber, a new type of very tough man-made material that is much stronger than metal. New planes built with carbon fibers—like the F-15 Eagle, F-16 Fighting Falcon, and F/A-18 Hornet—were sturdier than older ones.

These lightweight fighters were also fitted with electronic and computer systems that reacted more quickly than the pilots who were operating them. They had only one real weakness in flight: the pilots themselves! The strain caused by hard turns during an air fight would leave these planes undamaged, but it could knock a pilot out. Despite all the high-tech computers on board, the aircraft manufacturers knew nothing could replace the decision-making capabilities of a human pilot. The pilot had to stay.

They had to figure out a way to balance the needs of the pilot with the needs of the military. So, the United States Air Force (USAF) began looking to replace its new fighter jets. This led to the development of the F-22 Raptor.

Although the computers aboard the USAF fighter jets were state of the art, they could not take the place of a human pilot.

COLD START

The USAF first began to think about designing a new fighter back in the 1970s. At that time, America was in the grip of the cold war with Russia (then called the Soviet Union). This was not a typical war. No countries were invaded, no missiles were fired, and no battles were fought. Instead, America and Soviet Russia were locked in a battle of ideas—political and social differences. They hoped to avoid fighting, but many feared this would end in a nuclear war that would kill millions.

At the time, Soviet Russia's armed forces greatly outnumbered those of the United States. Air combat was one area in which America was determined to stay ahead. To do this, America would need total control of the skies. Russia was building newer and better fighters like the Su-24 Fencer. America needed a plane that could beat them. In April 1980, the USAF started the Advanced Tactical Fighter (ATF) program. They wanted aircraft that would be able to destroy the newest Russian fighters, plus any they might build in the future.

A HISTORY OF VIOLENCE

Planes were first used for combat at the beginning of World War I (1914–1919). Most of them were biplanes. They had two sets of wings and no guns. Pilots fired at each other with pistols they had carried with them on board the aircraft!

By the end of the war, there were real fighter planes, specially fitted with machine guns. Pilots, however, still sat in open cockpits exposed to cold and wind. They had to bundle up in warm clothes just to be able to fly.

TAKEOFF

The USAF held a competition to choose the ATF designers and engineers. In October 1988, two teams were invited to build prototypes, or models. They were Lockheed and Boeing, who designed the YF-22, and Northrop and McDonnell Douglas, who designed the YF-23. A competition for the engine design was also held. This was the largest fighter competition ever. It was worth billions of dollars to whoever won.

The USAF designed a tough set of exams and tests to decide the ultimate winner. It wasn't until April 1991–two and a half years later–that the Lockheed and Boeing YF-22 design was declared the winning aircraft. Pratt & Whitney's P&W F119 engine was chosen to power the YF-22.

HOW MUCH DOES IT COST?

The Raptor is the most expensive fighter plane ever built. Initially, the USAF gave aircraft manufacturers $10.91 billion to design the prototype and figure out how to build it. They also gave Pratt & Whitney, the company that

Workers paint the first operational F-22 Raptor to be delivered to the U.S. Air Force.

makes the Raptor's P&W F119 engines, $1.36 billion. Each plane is so costly that the fleet will have to be bought over several years. The full amount the government plans to spend on

buying the Air Force's newest set of fighters will be a total of $96 billion. Each plane costs over $133 million! Ka-ching!

The military uses radar such as this to find
enemy fighter planes and to guide weapons
toward their targets

THE INVISIBLE JET

Meanwhile, on secret military bases in the Nevada desert, the USAF had begun testing a brand-new technology called "stealth." Stealth was a new way of building warplanes so that radar could not spot them. At the time, this technology was top secret. The USAF wanted it on all their new aircraft. By the mid-1980s, all ATF manufacturers were being asked to include stealth in their airplane designs.

LOOK, UP IN THE SKY! IT'S A BIRD! IT'S A FIGHTER PLANE!

Although the F-117 Nighthawk is the most famous stealth fighter, it technically isn't a fighter. It is a bomber, a military aircraft designed to drop bombs on ground targets only. The F-22 is the first real stealth fighter. Not only is it designed for combat, it is very good at avoiding detection. It was named Raptor, a reference to birds of prey, in April

The F-22 Raptor is equipped to drop bombs in addition to shooting down other planes.

1997. The Raptor's mission is to shoot down other planes in addition to dropping bombs. It has even been built with new "smart" bomb technology. Smart bombs have built-in guidance systems to help them find targets with greater accuracy.

OUT OF SIGHT

Radar (**ra**dio **d**etecting **a**nd **r**anging) is a type of sensing device used to detect, locate, track, and recognize objects from far away. First, the radar sender shoots a burst of radio waves from an instrument called a transmitter. If the radio waves bounce back to the radar sender, then that means an object has been detected. The time it takes for the signal to bounce back to the radar sender indicates the distance and location of the object.

The Raptor's shape makes it difficult to find by radar. Many of its surfaces, such as the edges of the wings and its twin tail, are sloped. It also has sawlike teeth, like the edge of a steak knife, on some parts. These features help to scatter radio waves instead of bouncing them back to

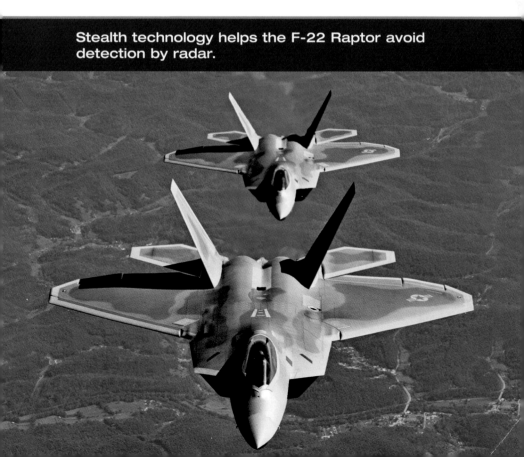

Stealth technology helps the F-22 Raptor avoid detection by radar.

the sender. Because the enemy receives no return signal, it cannot detect the Raptor.

Surfaces such as the nose, the forward edge of the wings, and the engine exhaust nozzles cannot be shaped to scatter signals. Instead they are painted with radar absorbent material (RAM)—a paint that absorbs radio waves.

TOP GUN

Stealth technology enables the Raptor to "see" a target and destroy it before it knows it has even been hit. This is called "first look, first shot."

The Raptor carries air-to-air missiles (AAMs) to use in battle. Each missile is stored inside a bay, or compartment. There are four bays. There is one on each side of the Raptor and

WHAT'S IN A NAME?

Why is the F-22 called the Raptor? The fighters that the F-22 Raptor is replacing are the F-15 Eagle and the F-16 Fighting Falcon. Raptor means bird of prey, such as an eagle or a falcon, so it's a good all-inclusive name for this class of fighter. Raptor is also short for "velociraptor," one of the scary dinosaurs in the highly popular film *Jurassic Park*. That movie opened around the same time that the F-22 was being named.

The F-22 Raptor can fire air-to-air missiles (AAMs) at targets that are many miles away.

two in its underbelly, or lower side. These bays are only opened when missiles need to be fired.

The Raptor carries two types of AAMs. It has six AIM-120C Advanced Medium Range Air-to-Air Missiles (AMRAAMs). These are stored in the underbelly bays. Two short-range AIM-9X Sidewinder missiles are housed in the side bays.

FIRE AND FORGET

The AIM-120C AMRAAM has its own radar, making it a "fire and forget" weapon. When a target is chosen, the Raptor's computers pass the information to the AMRAAM. Once launched, the missile uses its own small radar to home in on the enemy. It can attack from over 50 miles (80 km) away. Meanwhile, the Raptor can turn away and focus on another target.

The AIM-9X Sidewinder is a shorter-range missile used when the Raptor is entangled in a dogfight, or close-up battle, with an opponent. The 'Winder, as it's called, is another fire and forget weapon that uses heat to detect a target. Its radar homes in on the heat from an aircraft, usually the engine exhaust. Then it attacks.

It takes several soldiers to load the F-22's missiles into its weapons bays.

MISSILE CONTROL

The Joint Helmet Mounted Cueing System (JHMCS) directs the AIM-9X Sidewinder to its targets. The JHMCS is a type of gun sight fitted to the pilot's flying helmet. The 'Winder seeker head is the nose of the missile that is supercooled. This makes it extremely sensitive to heat and able to detect any that is being generated by an enemy aircraft. The seeker head is controlled by the JHMCS. When the pilot turns his or her head, the missile follows. In other words, the Raptor pilot can send a 'Winder at an enemy aircraft just by looking at it! The target is selected using the JHMCS. Once the Raptor's computers tell the pilot the 'Winder has the target in its sights, he or she simply fires. The rest is up to the missile.

FROM HERE TO BOMB BAY: AIR-TO-GROUND WEAPONS

Before 1997, the Raptor did not carry any bombs. That year it was upgraded so that it could carry bombs for the first time. The aircraft is now equipped to haul Joint Direct Attack Munitions (JDAMs). The JDAM is actually a kit that turns a normal gravity bomb into a smart bomb. Gravity bombs aren't always accurate. They lack guidance systems and can drift off course. That means they must be dropped with great precision, and that's not always possible.

With a JDAM kit, however, a gravity bomb can get an upgrade. Extra pieces like a new tail section give a normal bomb far greater range and flexibility. The little wings fitted as part of the kit allow a JDAM to be launched 15 miles (24 km) from its target.

The orange tail section and wing additions provide an instant upgrade to gravity bombs like these.

The kit also includes a satellite guidance system. This enables the bomb to hit within 40 feet (12 m) of the target. The Raptor can also carry eight Boeing small diameter bombs (SDBs). These bombs also use satellite guidance. Because the damage they cause is more contained, SDBs are used when there is a possibility of hurting innocent civilians or damaging homes or property.

chapter 3

IN THE COCKPIT

The Raptor pilot's office is the cockpit. It has far fewer gauges and dials than are usually found in an airplane cockpit. It uses six display panels that look like computer monitors. All information the pilot needs to know can be found on these displays. Another feature of the cockpit is night-vision goggles. These are special lenses that can be fitted to the pilot's helmet so he can see clearly by using available light from the night sky.

The cockpit's canopy, or cover, is completely see-through, and it's the first to be made from a single piece of material. It has no frame that can obstruct a pilot's view. Although it is see-through, it is not made of glass. It is made of polycarbonate, a type of very hard plastic. The pilot sits in an Advanced Concept Ejection Seat (ACES II).

The F-22 Raptor has the most advanced cockpit ever designed for a jet fighter.

He can eject, or make an emergency exit, from the Raptor if it ever suffers some sort of disaster. First, the canopy is launched clear of the plane. The seat unit–pilot and all–is then fired out of the aircraft with rockets built into the seat. Once clear of the plane, a parachute opens, the pilot separates from the seat, and he drifts down to safety. The pilot has an oxygen cylinder attached to his helmet, so he can keep breathing even if he ejects at a high altitude where the air is too thin.

NIGHT SIGHT

Night vision technology was created to locate enemy targets at night. It is also used for surveillance. Detectives and private investigators use it to watch people they are assigned to track. Many businesses and apartment complexes have cameras equipped with night vision.

Night vision can work in two ways. The first type is called image enhancement. This type of technology collects tiny amounts of light that are present but can't be seen by human eyes. The light is then increased to the point where an image can be observed. The second type of night vision uses thermal imaging technology. It detects heat from objects. This heat is reflected as light. Hotter objects such as human bodies give off more light than cooler ones like trees.

SKY CAPTAIN

When flying the Raptor, everything the pilot needs to know is shown on the Heads-Up Display (HUD). This is a 4.5-inch (11 centimeters) tall, see-through monitor on which vital information is projected. It can tell the pilot in which direction the Raptor is flying, how much fuel it has, where enemies are, and when weapons are ready for firing. The HUD sits on the edge of the control panel at the pilot's eye level. The pilot stays "heads up," which means he never has to look down into the cockpit to find out important information during the heat of battle.

RAPTOR ROUND YOUR FINGERS

The **H**ands **o**n **T**hrottle **a**nd **S**tick (HOTAS) control also helps the pilot stay heads up during combat. Like a joystick on a video game, it is used to steer the Raptor. The side stick is near the pilot's right hand. To the left are two throttles. They control the amount of power being delivered by the engines. There are various buttons on both throttles and stick that control up to sixty different functions. They can

The F-22 Raptor can soar at a maximum altitude of 50,000 feet (15,240 m).

do anything from changing radio frequencies to selecting the type of missile to be fired. These functions are vital in battle. HOTAS guarantees that the pilot does not have to fumble around in the cockpit during combat trying to find hard-to-reach switches. Everything he needs is right at hand. Each switch has a unique shape or texture so the pilot knows the difference without looking at them. Everything can be done by touch.

TRACK WHILE SCAN

The Raptor's "eyes" are its radar, the AN/APG-77 system. It is a much simpler design than older systems, yet it changes frequencies more than one thousand times per second to avoid enemy detection. It has fewer working parts and greater reliability, but much of what it can do still remains top secret. It can probably track targets from well over 115 miles (185 km) away. The radar is also able to control missiles. It can launch them at several targets at once while continuing to search for others. This is called "track while scan."

The F-22 Raptor's supercruise feature allows it to break the speed of sound without breaking a sweat.

chapter 4

THE NEED FOR SPEED

The Raptor is equipped with two Pratt & Whitney P&W F119 engines. Like everything on the Raptor, they are very advanced and more effective than engines currently used by other fighters. The engine parts are much tougher and do a superior job when compared to older engines.

The F119 also generates far more power than older engines. Each one produces 35,000 pounds (15,876 kg) of thrust (engine power). That's a lot of power considering that the engines of the USAF's current F-15s and F-16s only produce between 23–29,000 pounds (10,433–13,154 kg) of thrust.

All fighter engines use afterburners, devices that inject fuel straight into the engine's exhaust. This causes a sudden kick of power that quickly speeds the aircraft up. The fuel, however, is used up faster than normal. It also produces a lot of heat, which is easily detected by an enemy.

The Raptor's engines are so much better that they can supercruise, or fly at supersonic speeds, without using an afterburner. The F-22 can fly at a top speed of almost twice the speed of sound–over 1,400 miles (2,253 km) per hour–with its afterburner. The Raptor can achieve supercruise, which is its top speed, without afterburners, about 1,100 mph (1,770 km). This is 1.7 times the speed of sound! It makes the Raptor one of the first fighters to fly at supersonic speeds without using an afterburner. In fact, its F119 engines produce twice as much thrust without afterburners as older engines do using afterburners!

Supercruising allows the Raptor to use much less fuel than older F-15s and F-16s while going faster for longer. The Raptor can also stay in a combat zone for longer than older warplanes. Without the afterburner, it is also stealthier. There is no white-hot engine exhaust to give away the Raptor's position to heat sensors in enemy weapons. In addition, the F119 engine does not produce visible smoke like older engines. It leaves no smoke trail that can be seen by the naked eye.

These features alone make the F119 an excellent engine, but on the Raptor it has another feature called thrust vectoring. This allows the engine exhaust nozzles to swivel up and down, and this helps the Raptor to be much more agile. Using thrust vectoring, the Raptor can roll left and right 50 percent faster than with nozzles that point straight back.

BUILT FOR SPEED

The top speed of the Sopwith Camel, a fighter plane used during World War I (1914–1919), was 115 miles (185 km) per hour. In World War II (1939–1945), the P-51, below, could fly at 437 miles (703 km) per hour. The F-22's top speed is nearly 1,400 miles (2,253 km) per hour!

What lies on the horizon for the F-22 Raptor?

chapter 5

FUTURE FLIGHT

s there a future for manned fighters? As new technology and materials make planes tougher, stronger, and quicker, one thing becomes clear: it is the pilot who is still the weakest link. Why spend billions of dollars on a super-fighter whose capabilities cannot be fully used because they might harm the pilot?

What's to be done? There are two choices: First, change the pilot. Improve his brain and body's endurance so he can withstand more stress and fly future fighters safely. Of course, a human's endurance can only be improved so much.

Second, get rid of the pilot completely. Computers are getting better and faster all the time. They soon may be able to outthink and outfight human pilots. Unmanned fighters might be the wave of the future. Robot aircraft called Unmanned Airborne Vehicles (UAVs) already fly many missions. It is possible that the aircraft that eventually replaces the Raptor will have no room for a person on board. There might not even be a cockpit–just a very clever computer to do all the flying. By the middle of the twenty-first century, the USAF may no longer have human pilots. The F-22 might just be the last we see of the manned fighters.

Are fighter pilots destined to become a thing of the past?

F-22 RAPTOR
At a Glance

Forward fuselage

Cockpit

Duct skins

Side View

Wing

Empennage

Aft fuselage

Radar Absorbent Material

GENERAL CHARACTERISTICS

PRIMARY FUNCTION: FIGHTER/ATTACK	LENGTH: 62' 1" (18.8 M, 2.5 CM)
CONTRACTOR: LOCKHEED MARTIN	HEIGHT: 16' 8" (4.8, 20.3 CM)
ENGINES: PRATT & WHITNEY	WEIGHT: 60,000 POUNDS FULLY LOADED (27,216 KG)
COST: $133 MILLION (PRICE STILL TO BE DECIDED)	WINGSPAN: 44' 6" (13M, 15CM) CREW: ONE

NEW WORDS

afterburner (af-tur-**bur**-nur) a way of boosting power to an engine by injecting fuel straight into the super-hot exhaust

bay (**bay**) place inside a plane where missiles and bombs are kept

carbon fiber (**kar**-buhn **fye**-bur) a new type of very tough man-made material that is much stronger than metal

cockpit (**kok**-pit) the place in a plane where the pilot sits

fire and forget (**fire and** for-**get**) missiles that need no help with guidance once launched from the aircraft that fired them

radar (**ray**-dar) device that sends out radio waves that bounce off objects back to the sender and onto a display screen; used to see objects that are far away

raptor (rap-**tuhr**) a bird of prey

smart bomb (**smart bom**) a bomb that can be guided onto a target by either the plane dropping it or by using technology on the bomb itself

NEW WORDS

stealth (**stelth**) the act of being secret; meant to be hidden

supersonic (soo-pur-**son**-ik) faster than the speed of sound

technology (tek-**nol**-uh-jee) tools or machines used to make or do something

throttle (**throt**-uhl) the tool used to control the amount of fuel sent into an engine

thrust (**thruhst**) the force generated by the engine that is used to move a plane through the air

wingman (**wing**-man) the pilot of a plane that flies in formation with another

FOR FURTHER READING

Hansen, Ole Steen, and Alex Pang. *The F/A-22 Raptor*. Mankato, MN: Edge Books, 2005.

Miller, Jay. *Lockheed-Martin F/A-22 Raptor: Stealth Fighter*. Hersham, UK: Aerofax, 2005.

Green, Michael, and Gladys Green. Air *Superiority Fighters: The F/A-22 Raptors*. Mankato, MN: Capstone Press, 2003.

ORGANIZATION

National Museum of the US Air Force
1100 Spaatz St.
Wright-Patterson AFB, OH 45433
(937) 255-3286
www.wpafb.af.mil/museum/

RESOURCES

WEB SITES

F-22 RAPTOR STEALTH FIGHTER

www.f-22raptor.com/index.php
Visit the official site of the F-22 Raptor to learn
more about its history and special design
features.

U.S. AIR FORCE

www.af.mil
Learn detailed facts about the United States Air
Force. This site also contains links to F-22
Raptor related articles.

GLOBAL SECURITY.ORG

www.globalsecurity.org
This site provides news and reliable security
information as well as links to F-22 Raptor
related articles.

INDEX

INDEX

ABOUT THE AUTHOR

Steve White currently edits *Wallace & Gromit* and *The Best of The Simpsons* for Titan Comics. In his spare time, he continues to develop his obsession with sharks, dinosaurs, and The Simpsons.